THE GREATEST SUPERHERO

by Casey Head

illustrated by Lindsay Kemple

The Greatest Superhero
DeWard Publishing Company, Ltd.
P.O. Box 6259, Chillicothe, Ohio 45601
800.300.9778
www.deward.com

© 2016 DeWard Publishing

Cover and interior illustrations © 2016 by Lindsay Kemple

Design and layout by Albrecht Design

Printed in the United States of America.

ISBN: 978-1-936341-91-7

This book is dedicated to my six amazing children.
My hope and prayer is that you will
always put your faith in Christ.

THE GREATEST SUPERHERO

There once was a boy, who didn't fit in,
He was small for his age, with glasses, and thin,
The boys at school played football and wrestled,
They made fun of him, made him feel less than special.

One morning while watching his favorite cartoon,
Of the great Super Boy who could fly to the moon,
He had an idea that would make him a hero,
So that no one would ever again call him "zero!"

He ran out the door and looked up at the sky,
Then he jumped, and he jumped, determined to fly,
But whenever he jumped, he fell to the dirt,
There were grass stains and holes in his favorite shirt.

The door opened, and out came his dad with a sigh,
He sat down by the boy who had tears in his eyes,
"Why were you jumping, and why are you sad?"
The boy was too embarrassed to look up at his dad.

"I'm small and I'm weak, and I wear these big glasses,
When we play games like football, I drop all the passes.
I'm nobody special; Dad, I'm a zero,
I was trying to fly so I'd be a hero."

"I think I can help," said his dad with a grin,
"There's someone I know; he's my very best friend,
He made the earth and the stars; He made everything;
There's nobody like Him; He's the King of all kings!"

The boy dried his tears, "Dad, who is this guy?
Do you think he can help me fly high in the sky?
Then I'd finally be special, courageous and strong,
And I'd have lots of friends and really belong!"

"That's not how it works," said his dad, "But you see,
What He gives you is better, just listen to me:
If you'll love and obey Him with all of your heart,
He'll be your best friend, and that's just the start!"

"You see, there's this really, super bad guy,
Who wants everyone on this planet to die,
But my friend came to save us; He died in our place,
He died on a cross, alone and disgraced."

"But, dad!" Cried the boy. "How does that help me?
If He died and He's gone that's the end of the story!"
"Not really, son, because He rose from the grave,
He came back to life, to prove He can save!"

"My friend will not give you the power to fly,
But He can make you live, even after you die,
So in one way, that makes you a real superhero,
A child of the King, and never a zero!"

The boy thought for a moment, then lifted his face,
He looked up at his father, pondering grace,
"The same one who made the stars and the trees,
Came down to this earth to die just for ME?"

"Yes, my dear son," his dad whispered through tears,
"He loves you so much, so there's nothing to fear
And didn't I tell you, my friend's name is Jesus,
Because of His love, He saves and He frees us!"

"The one super power, the greatest of all,
Is the power to love, not to fly or play football!
He gives us a mission, to conquer the world,
By telling of Jesus, to boys and to girls."

14

The boy was amazed, he looked up at the sky,
It was then he gave up on the power to fly,
It was fine to have glasses, to be small and slim,
He didn't have to be strong to be special to Him.

"Yes, by God's grace, Jesus tasted death for everyone. God, for whom and through whom everything was made, chose to bring many children into glory. And it was only right that He should make Jesus, through His suffering, a perfect leader, fit to bring them into their salvation." (NLT)

Hebrews 2:9-10

Also from DeWard kids

Penny Sue the Pure Hearted
Serena DeGarmo

Join Penny Sue on her first Be-Attitude Adventure! What did Jesus mean when He asked us to be pure in heart? Penny Sue will find out when she comes face-to-face with a new girl at school who is rather prickly. Why is this person so difficult to get to know? Will Penny Sue be able to make friends with a girl who might be bad? Some things aren't always what they seem. See how God helps Penny Sue and see what happens with these two unlikely friends. ($7.99)

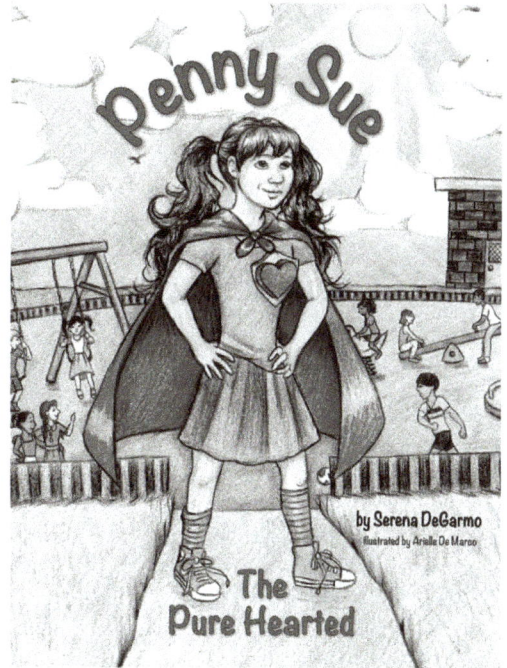

The Windkeeper
Emma Broch Stuart

Turn the pages and discover Wendall Windkeeper's purpose as he trains the four winds of heaven for their role in fulfilling God's greatest rescue mission-the birth of His Son. While *The Windkeeper* is fictional, God's purpose for each of us is very real. ($8.99)